Touching
Outer Edges

Collected poems by
Claire Possee

DEDICATION

My husband James Champion is always there, supporting me and cheering me on. He has given me the confidence and energy to produce this collection of poetry. He tells me daily that he is proud of me and I want him to know how proud of him I am too.

CONTENTS

CONTENTS
(CONT)

Chapter 1 - Battles

The Harm They Do

A supposed animal lover, leaving a dog
cowering in fear and pain.
An alleged responsible adult, causing
suffering to a cat they've claimed.
What goes through their minds?
They've no empathy for other creatures.
It can be sensed in the way they talk,
perhaps even in their features.

It chills me to the core, this abuse
of animals in all its grotesque ways.
The motives are unknown, unbound,
happening right under society's gaze.
Sentences meted out for maiming
or killing a defenceless rescue, stray or pet,
are never enough to compensate for
the harrowing hell we could forget.

What gives a man or woman the right
to beat or stamp on an innocent dog or cat?
It seems a weekly news item now
uncovering this truth from the domestic mat.
We should condemn all that lies before us:
the evidence we see from the underside.
No more looking the other way when it gets harder;
it should not be the truth that is denied.

Tougher jail terms are required for the
acts of harm to the vulnerable canine and feline.
Any rights the "owners" had for the keeping
of these creatures should be realigned.
People like that should not expect leniency
when they commit these vile crimes.
If we could educate them in the process,
this could diminish the vile times.

As a lasting thought to the animal-lover in most of us,
we have to battle this growing disease.
The one of lust for blood and disgusting thrills.
Let us shield all our pets from this unease.

Repaying the Debt

A policewoman carrying out her job.
A firefighter keeping us safe.
These people deserve consideration.
A mental health nurse
reducing us to tears as we watch
him at the very breaking point.

All viewed on the tv but this
is their reality not media hype,
or just a swipe at the government.
Hidden in their humble lives,
our protectors find they need
shielding from homelessness and hunger.

Listen as they unveil the untold:
Life is undervalued and so is thought and care.

It's not a truth that is convenient,
to those who want to reduce the police
and keep the emergency services overworked.
Nothing is relevant, only egos and echoes
of what has gone before.
And then lessons are not taken forward.

What is learned, though, is how
the policewoman has to endure the pressure
of living in one room with her child.
The nurse is limited in living too
his diet is pitiful, snacks in the cupboard
where there should be fresh food to sustain.

Shame could last a lifetime, words
could be the lifeline to these people.
They need action not token excuses.
A government on the right
could do the humane deed and pay
what is owed in pounds and promises.

No Spare Earth

Humans can deny and often lie,
Nature always tells the truth,
if only people could hit rewind.
It could be a small lifeline
thrown in the spirit of remorse
to a world being swallowed.

We don't have the luxury
of two Earths. We can't just call on
a spare like a tyre for our sacred
four-wheel drive car,
that would literally eat up the road,
the air, existence of all beings.

Profiteering of the planet seeps
and oozes into people's brains,
like an oil slick smothering sense.
Use items once, and never again
with no conscience and no
clue to where the items wash up.

The oceans choked and creatures
caught, tangled in a plastic web.
We did that, we should all wear shame.
This material we revere,
then attempt to bury in landfill,
fulfilling a need to 'move on'.

The youth of the year 2019
have jolted us back to reality
lifted our veil of complacency.
Their powerful protests
lining the streets of cities
defying the old egotists and deniers.

We're told we have very little time,
urgency is needed where
lethargy led us previously.
Wake up! Wake up to catastrophe
now it threatens our lives, our one
and only Earth. One pledge to make.

An Innocent Coffee?

A journey from bean to cup
is not just about the coffee
appearing to us, in innocence
it's more about the legacy.
The vastest of vendors
take pride in their stock.
What they miss off the list
comes as a great shock.

The moral microscope
focusses on farmers in Peru.
They hold the contracts over
the world through and through.
The lens picks out young
children and tender teens,
who climb through brutal
bushes to pick precious beans.

A wrong made worse by more
wrongs, as consumerism expands.
No-one can deflect their guilt,
as the blame is in all our hands.
We drink the coffee in the shop
not questioning the source,
while far off children ache
their suffering is enforced.

It is not a journey
into some forgotten era,
although this child labour
has now been made clearer.
Media coverage lays bare
the depths of inhumanity.
These images they portray
peel back to sheer insanity.

The madness and the cruelty
of enslaving ones so young,
marked out for scrutiny,
so we can save the unsung.
Stop before you think to drink
the takeaway coffee you bought.
We have to challenge the 'brands',
the greed and this non-thought.

A Bed in Covent Garden

A job can mean many things
and many aspects to a person,
security, self-esteem,
a sense of belonging here.
What it shouldn't mean
is having nowhere to rest
after several hours striving
without a real living wage.

A man you may have observed
educated, talented and bilingual,
who took on a role that
he could probably do in his sleep.
If sleep could occur in peace
with a roof overhead, instead
of the stars gleaming
in a cooling Covent Garden.

This European man who knows
London maybe too well, who tried
to escape the quicksand of
homelessness but slipped.
It's grip taking hold
only loosening when a hand
reached out, that of a female
reporter from a known TV channel.

This woman sought to assist him
to give him sympathy and wisdom.
As she had felt the sharp point of
deprivation, marking her mind.
Her childhood eaten up and spat out
by house-sharing; an innocence
dissolved by the domestic abuse
she heard through the walls of neighbours.

What cruelty spirals through life
and shames society's rule-makers,
the takers of these people's hours
never recompensing or returning time.
Woman and man, only two of many
thousands. A bed should be one small
token and a gesture, but the paid work
they do could be paid better, easing the toil.

The lasting image of this woman
conversing and reversing the trend
of denial and hypocrisy that
the man has encountered to date.
Burnt into the screen that relays
the collected truths and travesties
of lives for many on the streets
working but still treated shamelessly.

Divided by All Things

We know who is guilty:
those, who hide their eyes from you.
We can sense your sadness,
a shattering, all-encompassing grief.
The ones left behind after Grenfell,
the fire stole your families, your privacy.
Now the leaders, the governors of your futures
argue over who is to blame, who wears the shame.

This, a new warning of our age, draws a
stark line in the ashes of the aftermath.
The truth unravels from the deceits of many decades.
The truth is enough to wake our leaders from inertia.

The trust, the faith, the control
you thought you had in abundance -
it is shaken like the papers
on the council desks, awaiting attention.
Many questions falling from our lips
for you, with you, in solidarity.
How was this allowed to happen?
The most sobering query of them all.

The answers extracted slowly like teeth
mostly by journalists in their searching ways.
The assistance even slower still from officials,
though volunteers show their merits with humility.
Then dignified you rise and
pick up your lives, steel your hearts
against this terrifying and all too-real tragedy.
The pain gripping and not subsiding.

The images still turning and filling
the void of empty words, and the tasks to
be done are many-fold, we just want to hold
you close to us and give solace where it's lacking.
The wealth-laden in society can never feel this agony
not like you feel it; the damage has been wrought.
Lay anger at the doors of power and take
our strength with you on the path to justice.

Reading Rights

The United States:
that forward-thinking land.
Where opportunities are
rife, you would say.
Well no, wait, this
can't be right - did
you say some people there
can't read, let alone write?

Almost one in five face
every day never knowing
never experiencing
the language of reading.
A child deserves as much
to be able to shape the vowels,
the consonants in their mind
and out to the waiting world.

A basic human right
to have this skill, just
at their disposal; the child
and the adult alike.
But society has other plans
for the poorest, the forgotten.
a cruel blow to those already living
on dreams that will be crushed.

The city of Detroit,
her children hold this knowledge
feel it sharply. The tools of life
always denied them until...
A man here and a woman over there
aiding their learning at last.
A shaft of light
piercing the darkness of ignorance.

If not for these people
the child, the adult would be trapped,
eternally a slave to non-reading.
A slow journey to literacy unfolds.
Heroes from simply teaching
the lessons of life through words.
Those precious words written
and remembered with endless pride.

Love, As It Recedes

Earth rotates ever onwards, though
it is oblivious to humans and their crimes.
Exposed in the expanding universe,
the planet has some magic on its side.
A sleight of hand that is lacking
in our clumsy dealings with one another.
We allow greed, laziness and arrogance
to overshadow the delicate balance.

Wars still rage and flare, as the blue planet burns;
humans not caring to put out either flame.
Fuels exploited by all and every industry
and never considered as a finite gift.
Animals slain for their ivory, their skin and fur,
poachers making their profit from blood.
No love lost on those creatures with the bad luck
to stand between humans and their grisly gains.

This world could hold love, as much
as people could exchange while they rearrange
the hierarchy - perhaps so there was none at all.
A dream; made into reality, captured forever as Truth.
Yet humans seem to choose to dump love,
swapping it for indifference, self-satisfaction.
Dressing themselves in all the glory of falseness.
This is chilling to witness, and hard to justify.

A river of kindness could flow un-damned
from one person to the next with no effort.
Compassion, empathy and logic as liquid
assets could be carried on that river forever.
An ocean of tranquility could swell and
Sweep all humans to a new land of hope.
One that embraces all races, all nations:
nobody is left to perish or regress or regret.

All that is tangible, is visible now and maybe it
always has been though now we are fully aware.
Precious time has been frittered away while
the Earth burns and turns and tilts.
When we can be with love again it may not
be the end - just a different phase of wisdom.
One in which we learn to cherish not destroy.
One in which we see hate recede, finally.

Spiral of the Anti-social

Time has speeded up
it seems, making us
less aware of our dreams.
No longer conscious
of our conscience. Are we
now subject to others lies?

Social media has enabled
us to boast, to shout out
like shots from loaded guns.
In this quickening squall
of fake news and fake views,
we may teeter between worlds.

All the usual suspects of
social media are there
keeping us entangled and 'liked'.
We appear closer together,
however we feel not ourselves
as we move further from each other.

The stream of senseless
gossip and guilt-edged advice
wrapped up as a therapy.
Some digital medicine for
what seems to be inanity.
Leading us forever round, down.

We hold our lives in disregard
when we let this addiction
take us on the vertical.
Instant gratification is never
a true satisfaction
whichever way you slice it.

Close the laptop lid or turn
off the phone, or hide the tablet
to mute the cyber chatter.
Retreat finally from the screen,
let's walk in the chill air
inhale life as it manifests instead.

The Brain Leaving Us

What can we bear, the sorrow or regret
knowing we live with this burden of grey matter
that always matters, even when we can't use it
to do, think, be any more.
The person we are, and then the person we were
is magnified to our loved ones, our carers.
They will perhaps know the signs of our demise
and their hearts burn with anger against this cruelty.

The capacity to know and feel,
once sharp as the kitchen blade, the bathroom razor,
now blunted by our ageing and
the graceless onset of dementia.
We can bear this though as we have borne our lives
with the strength of light against the gloom,
our husband/wife/daughter/son or other
lifting us from the fog of loneliness.

It strikes where it can - the maddening whirl of
the disease at large is a fear and a force.
We can perhaps slow its pace at least
seek help, take the hand that grasps for us.
The threads that tangle and knot
in upon themselves, they are the thoughts
we had when we could explain our needs.
Now our needs are one hundred-fold.

The reality is no longer solid like glass.
The mind wants to shut down - let's fight the urge.
Hold that thought, remember our loved one's face
and keep it close to us.
For all our sakes let us not
lose the warmth, the passion, solidarity,
Our combined brainpower
may eventually beat this insult to dignity.

Chapter 2 - Close to Me

Visions of Avebury

A friend took me to see the place in Wiltshire,
it was a spontaneous visit.
We were not expecting any events
just some scenic views in the sunshine.
As soon as we drew up in her car
we could spy something unfolding;
it was an extra dimension
to the ancient stones of Avebury.

When we had taken in the sights
of the first field of aged rocks,
we crossed over to the other site
and in a sense we crossed worlds.
So we had become part of the crowd:
an audience for ceremonies and rites.
I was enthralled, felt warmed and strange
my friend stood amused, bemused.

It was when we quietly chuckled
at the people and their customs,
that I recognised one of those in robes
a man from my hometown in Hampshire.
In his other life he had engaged in politics.
But now it seemed the man planned
to get a different community
together there, to listen to his words.

Apart from this man there were others
being ordained by the chief druid.
Men and women clad in robes were
being blessed and presented to their peers.
A young man related a poem he'd written,
another promoted a music festival
in the hope of recruiting more players
some followers of the dreams the druids shared.

We took our leave not long after
and wandered to where more stones stood.
We talked, mulling over what we'd seen,
much in awe of the mysteries of Avebury.
The experience left me enlightened
a part of its magic, but also outside of it.
I knew my friend enjoyed the trip
as she grinned at me, and we walked on.

Copenhagen in June

Denmark calls for us so we take flight
into the arms of its capital.
My man and I have gone to sample
the smorgasbord, the sights, the life.
Staring us in the face is the much-needed
Andersen Bakery.
How then can we resist, especially it's super-sized
brunch sided by a latte.

The meal enjoyed we set upon the
inviting gardens of Tivoli.
What awaits us inside are all ideas fantastical,
realised in the magical.
Fairground rides, and candy-floss fumes,
offset by the rising fountains.
A palette of spring hues delights our eyes, with
blooms of dancing graces.

We're drawn in by the bird life too, the prowling
peacock surveying his grounds.
On another wander through the city,
we seek out the marvel of the Little Mermaid.
Her languid pose atop the rocks in her forever-domain;
waiting for her next photo-call.

Our two-day visitation in Copenhagen, nearly
at a glorious but too-quick end.
We climb aboard the ferry for a float around
the waterways, the old ways.
We draw comparisons with Amsterdam, while we
glide the path well-sailed.
Knowing though that this city has found it's
own culture, industry, it's pure heart.

Park Pleasures

The path passes through Eastrop Park,
tilting away from Basingstoke centre.
I'd call it a haven in the urban buzz
taking me away from the noise and fuss.
Seeking out some flora and fauna,
I find here it's not hard to unearth.
Dressed in racy red the tulips
are the first to take this stage.

The bobbing blackbird comes into view,
gracing me with his observance.
I watch as he flits through the foliage,
beak of amber, piercing the shadows.
His partner, she flies in further along,
swooping, then settling in the mown grass.
Her eyes keen, scouring the green for fuel.
I observe, absorb and move onwards.

The boating lake now in my sights,
under April skies scored by contrails.
Other people emerge on foot and bikes,
as the sun gains its mid-morning strength.
A pair of mallards alongside a solo coot
glide gently as I stride quietly by.
I sense the true tranquility of this park
it's breathing, it's feeding, it's intimacy.

Nature entwined with humans and their activity.
Life sustained and life passing through.
No better tonic than a walk around here,
where simple pleasures touch the senses.
To be renewed, regenerated and reset,
as though the park had worked a magic spell.
The homeward paces are filled with more
knowledge, more bounce and vitality.

Parisian Delicacies

Landing light on our feet, not fresh but eager to eat.
We could virtually taste the petit dejeuner as we
chose a cafe in the city sunrise.
Very little French had we, but it was no hindrance
to our order or our enjoyment,
drinking in the scenes and the coffee.

Taking a wander down through the streets,
our next destination the celebrated and feted tower
of Eiffel, how wonderful.
The winter had been banished
all but vanished from the bluest skies of Paris.
With the sun shimmering, leading us deeper in.

My fiancé navigated our route to the tower,
and as we found it wasn't far to gain the park,
the start of the grounds and viewing area.
The feeling of greatness in our midst,
and that many had seen this marvel of
architectural genius, came upon me then.

But we would wait until the evening to immerse
ourselves in the wonder of the metal and lights.

Coffee called to us, in our orientation of the city,
so we let that urge win, And so to begin anew,
we sought out our room for rest and refresh.
An apartment building in the civic quarter,
close at hand for all the major landmarks
and for all the adventures we could take in a weekend.

Later when we had fully revived ourselves
we returned to take on the tower, the queues were our
only low-point and no barrier to our tangible delight.
Looking at my beloved's face, when we as wind-whipped
tourists took steps on the viewing platform;
I experienced a chill, a thrill like a new-formed being.

A Whitchurch Walk

Briskly, my feet carry me
towards the park for lunch.
This is my daily walk-around
away from desk and phone.
I enlist all my senses here
in readiness to catch all aspects.
The wind-whistled streets,
flow from one to another, and on.

When I am seated in front of
the fenced fields, the stripped-bare trees,
I turn to observe the birds
who sing here, to lighten the air here.
Yes the robin is resident now
quite the manager of his grey terrain.
And then I hear the magpies caw
encircling me in their comforting din.

I stretch my gaze further out
to find more birdlife in the glare.
Winter sun breaking through,
cracking the glaze of January gloom,
The sparrows shoot through leafless boughs,
speaking in their chattering tones.
The peace is still upheld along,
while I finish my savoured lunch.

As quickly as I gained this spot,
I hurriedly vacate its varied virtues.
For a timely return to phone and desk,
to continue the afternoon anew.
A spring-clean of my thoughts,
And a strengthening of my body.
All good things are collected in
as the day's walk ends again.

Madrid Memories

Spain in September
with you, I remember
how we revelled in the sun
and laughed as we were one.
Our eyes were opened wide
when we queued, stepped inside.
Into the Museo Del Prado there;
the wonders were all to share.

Our room for two nights
was a haven from bright lights.
In the suburbs of Madrid,
we enjoyed all we did.
The delights of our city tour
encompassed food, drink and more.
Our walks in warm streets
on the search for top treats.

The memories I hold dear
when you and I are near,
take me all the way to Spain
to the beautiful domain.
Treasuring the hours
while we admired the flowers,
of El Retiro Park's array.
Let's return there one day.

Precious Hound

Memories of hairs in the house,
covering our floors, our sofa, ourselves.
The licking tongue of our contented
canine, her eyes glowing and all-knowing.
Unfiltered love between us
the rarest of treasured gifts,
which lifts the mood and enriches
the bond shared for countless seasons.

Walks were unhurried while
my retriever cross - with basset - sniffed
and savoured every blade of grass,
that wavered in the breeze, in our realm.
The minutes, hours of untroubled
strolling like there was no-one else
drifting by in our sun-soaked dream.
Just me and she gently living.

A frozen fragment of recall
where I see myself sleepily walking
down our stairs at my old home
and patting her warm, silken, furry head.
It's unrivalled, that longing
that sense of being out all day,
and yearning to connect with her
to touch her fur again and smile.

I'm not likely to ever forget
her sweet face, her spins and her place in my life.
Eternally with me, our Pepsi
her trusting eyes seeking mine and uniting our hearts.

Sardinian Sparkle

The beach-lover's retreat
the resort of Fertilia, jewel of Sardinia.
Walkers on the road from nearby Alghero
are embraced by the fragrant pines.
Swimmers ride the gentle waves
then pad onto silken sands.
The bleached driftwood forms
natural sculptures and symbols.

Even this heaven,
this sun-dipped gem
reveals a darker shade:
that of Mussolini.
The dictator
who put his mind to design,
The structures of residence
Leaving his imprint, his ideals.

And yet the pull of this place
is not diminished.
People of this century
engage in its eternal beauty.

Children laugh wildly
eyes locked onto the silver fish,
that slide under their limbs;
Their motion is hypnotic.
Chinese ladies appear on the dunes
to offer back-rubs to the visitors.
A few agree to have hands laid on
while they absorb the solar rays.

The Mediterranean flows on
refreshing the bay and its community,
refuelling energy
of all life in its grasp.

Friendship's Face

The bond of two is shared in evolving chapters:
sometimes the book of friendship
is read quicker than we would think.
With other companions we embrace each other
after months or years apart.
The healing of soothing words is sweet therapy.

What made us grin in youthful days
together as a fearless double act,
has faded with our many memories.
Those seasons where we shared all
with growing pains, and teenage gains
and no thought to the unknown future.

Discarded then our childish dreams
as we both look to life and love and
the need to flourish in our chosen sphere.
This connection deepens to the next level
letting us both experience laughter, tears
and telepathy, created only by the two of us.

The very epicentre of this unity
is empathy - your eyes look into mine and I look
straight back in understanding of your words.
I am touched by your actions when you know
others may scorn me or dismiss my thoughts.
Always my picker-up, forever my sister-in-arms.

We'd never stand to lose each other
only strengthen our ties and our hearts
with every cherished moment that elapses.
I sense you will be with me forever, even
when we may be parted by miles, always
those smiles will be as natural as breathing.

Four Legs, Two Wheels

The two of us, on two wheels, rode to our chosen destination.
Moving through some of Holland's finest earth, water and cultivation.
A journey on our bike twenty kilometres north of Volendam, our town.
The end-point of Hoorn, we'd heard it had a sublime air and a harbour of renown.

My fiancé put in the effort and peddled us along the route to see this place.
The sun seared the clouds as he wheeled and navigated us with an even pace.
Me, the observer, the pre-warner of traffic behind and beside him and me.
The fresh and adventurous image we created, we were our own entity.

Throughout our traverse we encountered a varied selection, a collection of delights.
One of these was an unseen person, gliding by and even sliding by in our sights.
Their vehicle, a capsule so unusual and bizarre, it made us start to laugh.
In all it's yellow coating this bob-sleigh with wheels was a wonder and a half.

Arrival at Hoorn meant lunch at a boutique bakery: prime panini and a coffee.
We observed the crowds, the shoppers, all absorbing the air, the sun and sea.
We launched ourselves among those crowds to experience the heady atmosphere.
Vintage cars surrounded us and the town filled with sights so rich and sounds so clear.

Best of these images and resonant noises that we captured in our mind's eye:
The smart and imposing harbour, Hoorn's hub framed by the azure sky.
The trail home was swift and uneventful but for one comical and chaotic scene.
Some cows were being herded slowly, to their farm, we could tell they weren't keen.
We were taken aback but smiled at their progress, their movement on the road.
This was our trip's finale imprinted on our memory, one ever-ready to re-load.

Chapter 3 - Natural & Spiritual

Soul Revival

Colours in the sky
ethereal, yet real as life.
I stare out in wonder
on this magnificence.
How can there be
blood red, fire-orange?
The hints of pink
just tainted with the black.

Beauty surrounds
this place, so balmy and still.
I come to rest here
to breathe, to think, to be.
Secrets under the sun,
lovers smiling as one:
they know this place exists
to give sensual pleasures.

The sands
under a setting sun,
My body
feels what has begun.

With every fibre
of my being, every pore,
I sense this beginning
as the shades slide away.
Darkness a cloak
to cover the silken sky,
No coldness though
As I wait for the night.

The sea
under a dusky sky.
My soul
Tonight will fly.

Lunar Longing

I've always felt its presence
enlivening me, that moon.
Making me look up night
after night, and in the daylight.
Though the force is not
threatening, it scares me slightly.
How can it still be presiding,
still shining and mesmerising?

I won't relay the hackneyed
phrases, or tributes to the moon.
It deserves more than that,
it warrants some silken sounds.
I imagine the chill of the
lunar surfaces and ridges.
I crave it's endless and
weightless state of mind.

Simply to touch it's hallowed
soil, if it is so-called,
would be the ultimate prize:
the bronze, silver and gold.
I envisage laughing in
space, at the place I fill
within the atmosphere.
High on the tranquility.

The moon as the stabilising
medium, in this too-fast
spinning world of dreams
and escape, and yet, mistakes.
The mysteries delicately
unfurled, not ripped apart.
So that I can slowly
inspect, digest and record them.

Yes, I can carry the secrets,
and transcend the lunar longing.
Protect the essence therein,
preserve its majesty for all.

Salute to the Spider

Witnessing the webs
all spun in silver thread.
Their beauty heightened
by the September mist-bed.
Noticing the intricate
nature of their creation,
I am in awe of the
makers of this sensation.

A myriad of spiders
match the multitude of designs.
Cleverness does not come close
to describing these finds.
I peer in at one such
industrialist in place,
Breathe down into the
network it has set in space.

We shouldn't fear
the arachnid like we do,
As we can see how small
it is compared to me or you.
Why then do we persist
in shuddering when it scuttles near?
We must know it won't bite
Poison, or kill, so it's just futile fear.

On behalf of the
spider population,
I'll give humans
some re-education:

Here's what I'd relay
about our eight-legged friends,
I would tell you not to fear
the way that each leg bends.
Remember that they eat the flies
and give us beauty to view each day.
They make the landscape more inviting,
spinning those webs in a wondrous way.

The Bohemian Way

Rejection of the norm
but no reflection on our shared life,
just a burning need
that we have to cast aside the strife.
Expectations of a world waiting
have weighed us down for too long.
We desire something more
a new outlook that is strong.

The channelling of our creativity
is the aim and our fuel,
for the fire that burns so bright
But also keeps our cool.
Someone says it's too hard,
setting up a business – let alone abroad.
What about our finances
and have we thought of local accord?

They can talk on and on
about how tough this route is,
but we will not listen
the deal is sealed with a kiss.
A change in direction because
we need the varied road,
That which we must take
to unburden and unload.

So we are heading for the finer life
one which will enrich and enlighten us.
There may be tough times there
but you and I are clever, ingenious.
Let's stay true to this path
For it's all we have dreamed of,
it is lined with the gold
that which is made of pure love.

Trick of the Night

A tortuous trek, a continual upwards climb:
this path that is seemingly unending.
Our journey towards the reward
of sleep that we never can attain.
The unfolding path appears inviting
at once teasing us and taunting us.
Those who tread upon its track
promised rest but delivered zero respite.

Some of us try to climb the gradual
incline or is it a moving escalator?
Whose sacred steps sliding
ahead just another numbing reminder.
Others awake among us pace their rooms.
Waiting for the walkway to quieten
and flatten out for an easier passage
onto the end-goal of silken slumber.

The collective mind won't free itself
from the day's events, either pleasing or not.
Therefore the line can't be crossed
from this active realm to one of calm.
Eternal dilemmas form like parasites
feeding off the sufferers' distress.
These shape themselves into solid blocks,
like barriers on the cerebral plane.

Is it better to ride the wave
of worry, or to rise above its crest?
To make the body and mind be still
or to activate and energise for future rest?
Would a remedy so traditional
as a milky drink and a book help then?
Could it fight the instinct
to lay wake in the nerve-shredded den?

The questions dissolve as morning
shakes us all out of night's hiding-place.
The jumbled-tumbled thoughts flood forth
and now it's too late, we are switched to "on".

Glory of Sleep

Nestling and settling
in the comfort of your bed
you wind away from the
day, from the buzzing in your head.
Cradling into the crisp
new sheet, under cool duvet.
Everything is set for sleep
that glory is gliding your way.

Within uncounted minutes
your body drifts, your mind too,
the wondrous waves washing
away all thoughts controlling you.
The brain being cleansed
as if by magic fingers,
rubbing away all the stresses
ensuring nothing lingers.

Rapid eye movements then
meaning you're dreaming with ease,
if only you could catch those
visions, put them in the deep-freeze.
Unfrozen they could play out
for your pleasure anytime,
dreamscapes filling your days
with the bizarre and the sublime.

Those waves of relaxation
taking you on nightly escapades,
rejuvenating your soul,
as each image subsides and fades.
When all that sleep is spent
and your waking is in no doubt,
you have attained your goal
the day sweeps you up and out.

Hotel Hideaway

I carry it with me
like a mobile or a half-cherished memory,
the hotel that haunts
only in the subtlest of intimate ways.
I want to get lost
in countless corridors.
Never found by fellow guests,
never followed by any staff.

This structure of my creation
keeps swallowing me whole.
I am consumed by the dream
my choice, my mind-space-time.
A place palatial and expanding
but also tightening at every turn.
The fibres of my dream
yielding only when I touch walls.

The need to embrace
all of these beginnings,
and all the endings, in rooms
is one I cannot resist.
I find a niche, in my
glowing golden bedroom.
The queen-sized bed a
clue to the comfort within.

No-one saw this, my
single sanctuary on the
second floor, they missed it
behind the unlocked door.

Architecture of my imagination
set in the reserve of the
melting mind.
So how long should I remain?
Leaving is also good but I
don't wish to right now;
not when I can bathe in the
blissful brightness of this frame.

Out on the Tightrope

Whoever took that initial step
and felt the shiver and shake,
they know the first flavour of freedom,
purest liberation.
The one person, now the many others
striding and providing
the power for their bodies
to take countless more steps.

Possessing the will to persist and seeing
that it's worth the risk. All adventure is in reach.
Marathons are run, through climates
cold and through searing heat.
The competitors vary in age,
but all hold that goal so bodily close.
A parachute opens in the bracing air,
meaning another woman or man faces nature.
.

The tightrope test is the method,
teaching every daring person
their strengths and shortcomings:
Humanity can be frailty.
Entrepreneurs use their energy,
alongside their minds, and perhaps designs.
It's that eye for the intricate
and the chance to display their calling.

The rush that fills the system
when a person with special knowledge
Engages and retains the custom of someone
on the path of a perfect purchase.
Dreaming of the tight-rope is one thing,
walking the real line is the essence of balance.

Fear of No Eternity

To truly grieve, to allow sadness
to engulf us is
as natural as breathing.
So why do we suffocate the feeling?
There could be a simpler way
than trying to push back the tide
of emotions and raw reality,
when someone we love leaves us.

A mortal light is turned off
replaced by a sheer darkness,
a blank of nothingness.
A person we cared for has left this world.
There is no mystery, and there is
only loss but still we are
not lost, just marooned briefly
to tend our hearts collectively.

Unlock the gate to all feelings -
guilt, melancholy, regret.
Release the fullest respect for
our fellow humans who are taken.
We cannot heal, without observing
the abyss while knowing the destiny
of everyone, no matter their status
and no matter the life they've led.

It may be the fear of that unforgiving
chasm that we would fall into,
that could swallow us all whole
keeping us hostage to denial and delusion.
It could be the worry that we
need some God to instruct us and entrust
special knowledge to our grieving
while we ignore our innermost thoughts.

Turn away from the old beliefs,
the reserved restrictions of the
stiff upper lip and the hushed tones
of the ceremony and customs.
Unlearn the muted way of Englishness
that binds us to being closed and alone.
Shake off the claustrophobic air
and embrace Death's true meaning.

Led by Ghosts

I walked down my staircase
it's spiral structure
keeping my mind alert.
As I slowly descended
I sensed some calming presence.
Not within, but out in the air.

Even now I can't label it,
or pinpoint it only to say
as I started to feel I was falling,
I had sensed a strong pair
of hands stretch out from
the afterlife and hold me still.

When I placed my foot
on the bottom stair, I could
hear some pleasant chuckling.
This was followed by a swift
release of aromas, filling
my whole sensory cache.

The cache was now full of these:
traces of mud and hay,
wafts of vanilla and coffee grounds.
The peculiar piquancy and mix
of the elements undiluted
drew me finally to the floor.

Layers of laughter engulfed
me then, like clothes made of
alien fabric yet feather-light.
My inner detective spoke
trying to piece these clues
together, compiling evidence.

41

Only at this pivotal thought
did I notice my body morph and
move without my brain leading.
Hostage of benign captors
I was taken, shaken,
forced to follow their cries...

On waking in streaming
sunlight and the chill in a
stripped-bare bed,
I knew it had been no dream
but a visitation from across
the metaphysical ravine.

Chapter 4 - Inspirations

Inspiration for 'Divided by All Things':

On 14 June 2017, an event happened in London that devastated many families and saddened the nation. Grenfell Tower in North Kensington was the scene of a terrifying blaze that eventually killed 72 people and injured many others. The disaster was so cruel and heart-breaking.

In my poem 'Divided by All Things', I wanted to convey not only the gravity of the event but also the anger that I felt for those who lost their lives and the families left behind to grieve. We now know that the cladding that had been put on the building was cheap and extremely flammable. We also know that many people who lived in the block of flats came from ethnic backgrounds. They were living in one of the wealthiest areas of the UK. And yet I believe they were treated appallingly and living in a death-trap. The sense of injustice and lack of answers haunts me to this day. I felt it necessary to underscore this anger with sensitivity and to praise the people who were, and still are, fighting to get answers and justice.

We will all wait to see if the families of the victims eventually get some closure, whenever this will be in the future. My hope is that they can create a movement of change, so that this will never happen again.

Inspiration for 'Innocence Melts Loneliness':

I had been watching a fantastic programme on Channel 4 in 2018. It was called 'Old People's Home for Four Year Olds', and I think it is televisual genius. Its premise was a social experiment to see if partnering young children with older people improves their lives and abilities. The experiment was done within an old people's residential home in Nottingham.

What struck me about this programme the most was the simplicity of the idea. Of course, the setting up, with all the attendant experts and assistants, was not a simple process. But the crux of the concept was beautiful and truly heart-warming. I think we all need to feel part of something, from when we are young and learning about the world to when we are in our golden years. We are all still learning and growing. Mainly it's about keeping our humanity burning as a positive force.

In my poem 'Innocence Melts Loneliness', I wanted to distil the essence of the programme with its ensuing benefits. It felt right to focus on the sweetness of the children and their effect on the senior citizens. This purity made such a difference to the older people's lives. In trying to capture the emotions and the outcomes of the experiment I brought the positive energies to the fore.

Inspiration for 'Repaying the Debt':

In 2018 I had watched a very moving and dismaying programme about people who work in the emergency services. This was on Channel 4 and part of their Dispatches series. The episode set out to explain the reasons why some police officers, ambulance workers, nurses and mental health professionals are struggling to make ends meet. I was shocked to see some on the breadline. This is why I chose to write 'Repaying the Debt'.

My idea was to relay how these people who dedicate their lives to their jobs in the emergency services are not being properly reimbursed. This means in money but also in quality of life. The police officer who is crammed into one room with her child - how is this right? As with some of my other poems I felt an injustice at how, at a basic level, these good citizens are being badly treated and forgotten. I appreciate there is more than one reason why, but I strongly feel that more needs to be done to highlight their plight and to rectify this unacceptable situation.

Inspiration for 'Trick of the Night':

I am a light sleeper - I can't get away from that fact. I know others are like me and find that sleeping is an uphill climb most nights. Whether it be trying to get to sleep, or falling asleep and then waking up frequently, this state is like a trick on our brains. I tackle this subject in 'Trick of the Night'.

I characterise this long journey into the night as 'the gradual incline' and it does eternally feel like that. I wrote this poem to soothe my mind, but I also wanted it to be cathartic for anyone who has sleep problems. A group therapy maybe. It seems we are always looking for answers to the problem of sleep.

If we can get a handle on why we aren't sleeping and how our brains are being muddled by the lack of good rest, perhaps we can move onto long-term solutions. I feel that sleep is directly connected to mental health and it is particularly pertinent in these difficult times of 2020. Dreams might unlock some of these issues - please refer to my other poems 'Hotel Hideaway' and 'Glory of Sleep'. These show the flipside of the old worries of lack of slumber.

Inspiration for 'Out on the Tightrope':

I wrote this poem in response to what I perceive as an admirable quality in people, that of the ability to take risks and push the self to achieve greatness. It is something I have learnt to do, after what seems like almost a lifetime of procrastination and "playing it safe". It always seems easier to say no and not take a leap into the unknown. It's one part fear, one part pride, and the remainder plain old bloody-mindedness.

I have a creative and supportive husband, who has taught me that taking risks is not a scary notion. It's a natural progression, an evolution of our ideas. We learn from doing - this has become our motto. I think it's a good mantra for life, and for every person who wants to have a fulfilling life.

When I speak of risk in the poem, I am addressing all risks: emotional, physical and financial. There are what we all face or choose to encounter, it's how we react to them (or not) that helps to shape our character.

I favoured the tightrope imagery because, to me, risks seem like they are always a fine balancing act. You are out there, almost on thin air, feeling your way from A to B. You have probably calculated the risk to a sensible degree but there are no real guarantees. It felt correct to characterise the risks as encountered by anyone, from sportspeople to business owners and beyond. It is the sensations and the bodily reality of taking risks that I wanted to explore.

ABOUT THE AUTHOR

I was born in Aldershot in 1973 and have lived in Hampshire most of my life. I grew up with an appreciation of poets such as Pam Ayres and Roger McGough. I started writing poems and prose in my teenage years, mainly to get my feelings and observations down on paper. Some of my inspirations have changed over the years but there are three areas I am always drawn to: injustice, travel and nature (of humanity and the outside world).

I'm quite a private person so I had never considered exposing my poems to that 'outside world' until recently. I think writing for me is a therapy and letting the words form themselves on the page is a release. My main hopes are to always be true to the subject matter, and to perhaps conjure up some images that may not be expected.

02/01/202

Dear Emma,

I hope you enjoy reading the poems in this collection.

Thanks, as always, for your eternal support and friendship.

Love from Claire
xx

Printed in Great Britain
by Amazon

54054186R00037